D0746348

DEC 13 2020

ROADVIEW LIBR

NO LONGER PROPERTY OF
SEATTLE PUBLIC LIBRARY

STEPWELL

AZURA TYABJI

NO LONGER PROPERTY OF
SEATTLE PUBLIC LIBRARY

I wish this book to be a well of reflection and sustenance.

Copyright © 2019 by Azura Tyabji
Cover Art By Julia Ismael

All rights reserved. No part of this publication may be reproduced,
distributed, or transmitted in any form or by any means, including
photocopying, recording, or other electronic or mechanical methods,
without the prior written permission of the author, except in the case
of brief quotations embodied in critical reviews and certain other
noncommercial uses permitted by copyright law.

The Seattle Youth Poet Laureate is a special program of
Seattle Arts & Lectures in partnership with Urban Word

ISBN 978-1-949166-01-9

Published by Poetry NW Editions
2000 Tower Street
Everett, WA 98201

Distributed by Ingram

PRINTED IN THE UNITED STATES OF AMERICA

STEPWELL

AZURA TYABJI

CONTENTS

STEPWELL

What To Do on Bad Days

find what you can change

you are not disappointing anyone
you do not have an expiration date
you are already equipped
with all the tools needed to sustain yourself
you cannot help but make magic.

Whitey's on TRAPPIST-1

after Gil Scott Heron

Recently, NASA discovered 7 earth sized planets orbiting a single star 40 light years away

One.
Another black woman
has crumbled to take a bullet in record time again.
There is no spaceship named after her.
We forget she had a name outside of bulk order eulogy.
Meanwhile,
Whitey is 40 light years away
making history in the way white men
love to be the fist to tame something that is content with being left alone.

Whitey has dreams of more heroic adventures
than his name being remembered after the funeral.

Two.
Ben Keita is lynched in Lake Stevens
and Whitey is 40 light years away.
He's terraformed his new planet by now, grown trees unhaunted by a black boy's neck.
All the fruit that hangs here is cruelty-free.
History too heavy to ship so
Whitey left it behind.

Three.
The families of all the Black kids gone too soon
turn their faces in the pictures towards the wall as Whitey lives a new slate.
One step for mankind, but we
are stuck 3/5ths of the way.
So why applaud a white man for doing what he does best?
Gaslighting our trauma to fuel his spaceships?

Four.
The Keystone XL Pipeline starts running and Whitey is 40 light years away.
He has discovered unfrozen water,
dips his feet in a lake as compliant as a mirror.
The long drink goes down easy, but
starts to blister his throat with lead and oil.
Rashes bloom angry with nostalgia on his skin and he thinks he's learned what it
is like to starve
to have a planet set against you,
reach into a well and lure only up
betrayal.

Five.
Whitey is drowning in lead and don't this feel familiar?
He is on some other hero's leftovers
This planet too, has nothing left to give.

Six.
Meanwhile back on Earth,
America has crumbled under its weight.
History too heavy for the flag to fly straight anywhere but a funeral.
We have decades of mourning
and centuries of healing.

Seven.
Whitey returns to Earth thirsty for forgiveness and we turn his ass away.
We don't need him no more and we be damned
if we let him appropriate this joy.

In our renewed Earth,
we have forgotten the language for "thank you, officer."
We have dissolved his borders, broken his prisons, and blocked his revolving
door of oppressors.

Here
the water is *good* again.
In it we have baptized our families with names more sacred than criminal.

Here
every brown kid is a star worth wishing on and every black girl
a sun so bright she can never go missing—
and Whitey
asks how much
a ticket back to Earth cost

and we say
"we don't need your money no more."
We've burned it all for warmth, but
mostly for
fun.

We ask
"what are you willing to give back?" instead.

We are the reparations at the center of the universe
And Whitey
is 40 light years
away.

NOTICE OF PROPOSED LAND USE ACTION
TO REPLACE THE YOUTH JAIL

NOTICE OF PROPOSED LAND USE ACTION

Master Use Project #: We have earned far beyond the numbers you put on our backs, so much that we are unquantifiable.
Address: 1211 E Alder St
Applicant Contact: the first time you were sent to the corner as a child, where the zenith of walls became a bent scale convincing you were the heaviest burden

TO CONSTRUCT A 1,742 SQ FT COMMUNITY CENTER AND MUSEUM HONORING LIVES DIMINISHED AND/OR LOST DUE TO INCARCERATION. THIS IS AN OPEN FLOOR PLAN, AS THE EFFICACY OF BORDERS HAS BEEN DISCONTINUED (SEE MUNICIPAL PLAN F45-FR). EVERY WALL IS MODELED AFTER THE QUILT YOU SLEPT ON AS A CHILD. INCLUDES EXTREME EXTERIOR AND INTERIOR ALTERATIONS TO OUR CURRENT STRUCTURE OF INJUSTICE AND AMNESIATIC CRUELTY. CONSIDER THIS A MONUMENT OF APOLOGY, A MEMORY SET IN PLAQUE, ITS CHILDREN NEVER SET BEHIND STONE AGAIN.

The comment period ends when the last white liberal runs out of excuses, but may be extended in the event of reparations. To submit reparations, say (and pay) "i see you" to pain previously sentenced to invisibility. Be sure to believe a young person when they say they know how to best treat the wound you gave them.

Rosé in Concrete Becomes New Flavor at the Pressed Juicery

White yuppies pour charitable ration of rosé
into their newly-paved
red carpet.

Wait for their gentrified libation
to summon a black-ish gurlfriend
into travel brochure.

They will drink her resilience dry
while praising how it makes their new palate,
their new dog-walking circuit,
their new neighborhood so
flavorful, hip, cultured, and *interesting.*

Before you get the ugly kind of mad and mourning,

they donate 1% of their profits to the hood's wake fund *(b-corp certified, by the way, if you know what that means) (and it's fair-trade organic) (they gave me 10% discount, just for living here, how nice is that!)*

Pink faces circlejerk
toasts around their tables.

It's *such* an honor
being the prized bull in their china shop.

To lower my haunches and look the trend,
be complimented on how
articulate
I swallow their language,

how different
from the other cattle I am,

how motivated I am to march

(so passionate!)

towards their waving, red flags.

Giants

From the sandboxes of construction sites,
kids scoop stolen heirlooms
from quicksand, suck the cement

from mixers and blow it like gum
POP!

There's a new hood.

We carve our eager heights into the tallest pines.
We use skyscrapers as full length mirrors and twirl
in our mama's *loudest* heels.

We snatch the air of helicopters like mosquitos
and hot potato bulldozers
in the schoolyard.

We doubledutch power lines to keep our lights on,
keep the city's heart skipping
a beat to catch up to our *gargantuan* glow up.

Lounging on the porches of ports,
swing our feet and there's the tides.
Tell a yo mama joke and there's a creation myth.

Everybody got "the Great" suffixed to their name now
for all we have survived! For all Lilliputian evil
we have triumphed above, and kept

growing! And when one of us cries,
no one can ignore it
because there's the rain.

When one of us dies, it takes all the white
chalk to draw us to the pavement,
by the time they're done

they don't have enough to kill another one of us so
we make chess pieces from their monuments.
We get extra loud in grocery stores.

We have big, big mamas and colossal homies
and there's enough for all of us!

There's enough for all of us.

There's enough for *all* of us.

You think there wouldn't be,
but there is.

206

Fusing the tender spot on my skull
was the first defense mechanism I learned.
Above me, buildings fused
into barrel chested giants
shivering hollow in the wind.

"The skull is an amphitheatre," grandma says.
When I was still young in South Lake Union,
I cradled a fallen sparrow's head
in the tenderness of my palm.

Beyond the endless breadth of my front yard,
a concrete orchestra swelled
in a pitch I couldn't yet hear.
I still speak to birds in whispers
when I chase them from crumbs.

I used to try slamming the door to pull the tooth,
but slacked my wrist before impact, every time.
On picture day, blood-gummed and grinning, a spoiled classroom
slowly emptied in my mouth.

The other girls used to say,
"you can't play with us because you're poor
and your skin isn't the color of glass."
So I huddled in the sandbox, prayed for fire,
and finally blended into the corner.

Still, the tide found me.
It rises higher every year, flushes
whole kids into different worlds,
only looks at them
through the rearview mirror.

To keep the monsters from crawling up
and taking me in the night,
I used to stuff the border between my bed and the wall with pillows.
By the time I realized their threats were imaginary,

there was a broken trench of rosaries
underneath my comfort,
scribbled treaties crumpled
like receipts and thrown
away.

When I got older, I chased after the guy
everyone else wanted.
I wanted to be his home so badly I eviscerated
my bedroom into a vacant lawn.
Crushed pots on my forehead and became the soil,
concussed confetti raining from my plea
asked over and over

"am I enough?"
"am I enough?"
"am I enough?"

"for you to take root here and stay?"

Some of us learn to stand taller by kicking.
Some of us learn to stand taller by spinning in funhouse mirrors and August smoke.
Some of us learn to stand taller through rumors, gusting around us like a magic carpet.
Some of us learn to stand taller by holding life hostage
in a steel drum and leading the marching band alone.

City grows up cold shouldered
stutters in and out of straight lines
and a wobbling compass towards home.

She doesn't text her parents when she gets there,
just scrapes her heels on the doormat
and falls into a restless sleep
she wishes someone will wake her up from.

206 bones are left in the body after development runs its course.
What a year of years its been.
She grew so quickly, her shins splintered.
Her head magnified and fractured,
pooled estuaries in a single tear.
She devoured a mic and busted her lip,
tried waltzing with phantom limbs
of communities that have since taken flight.

Where this city of growing giants and I will go from here,
I'm not certain.

I hope we give our word and stick to it
I hope we grow tender enough, again.

My love (noun.) is

1. grateful floorboard flooding,
2. bating breath before the dive is
3. always late to the destination or
4. always too early,
5. getting lost on the journey either way.
6. too precocious an ascetic,
7. chasing solitude but always taking the bait of
8. pedestals, the moon close to fullness mistitled as such,
9. inventing its own off-kilter orbit,
10. making waves nonetheless.
11. crucifying itself on a hook,
12. throwing "i love you" like a penny wish down
13. a well it cannot see
14. the bittersweet bottom of.
15. never losing faith in torn sleeves despite
16. outgrowing its first baby steps.
17. neither orphan nor prodigy
18. cautiously footsying with enlightenment,
19. learning how to trust its own worth, forever.

I might not have been my first love, but I will be my most everlasting.

Bee/Wasp/Butterfly

Pacific Science Center, Seattle, WA

Bee

The Pacific Science Center hive failed to overwinter.

a carpet of carcasses cover the floor,
husks of bees embalmed with dust,
a windowsill graveyard of everyday taxidermy.

The kids and I bought a ticket expecting vibrancy
after overwintering ourselves.
We take an un-celebratory moment
to mourn the dead drones,
workers, and queen.

A single bee will produce only ½ a teaspoon of honey before it dies.
When I make my tea, I stir
6 lifetimes
into my cup.

Wasp

"What's the use of wasps?"
Were they made angry?
Did God one day stub Their toe and out flew a
physical embodiment of bitterness?

All it takes to provoke a wasp
is sudden movement, like
bugging one of her friends
or summer.

All bees who sting are female.
A yellow jacket vendetta, fitting,
we also feel threatened when we are just trying to get a drink,
protect our friends, our exist.

Our defense mechanisms also can cost us our lives.

Why do I feel entitled for her to serve me sweetly?
Privilege melts easy on my tongue,
tastes like lifetimes.

Butterfly

Hundreds of butterflies are trapped in the ceiling net,
flayed out color baked by the spring sun and manufactured tropical heat.

I was here with a girl once,
praying our relationship would be less two awkward cocoons
and more two graceful butterflies.
That's what coming out is supposed to be, a joyous second birth.

I pulled the net in too soon to catch pride.
I did not break through the closet as triumphantly as a cocoon.
The colors I waited so anxiously to parade
didn't grow in as vibrant as I wanted.

In a gallery of gestation, dozens of cocoons hang in various stages of birth.
There are not many places you see a creature so fragile
born a second time.

"Exotic women and where to find Us"

tangles of our curls   gripped inside fists
compulsions   men down to cure   their yellow,   jungle fevers.
24 hour live   cams   unhindered   by timezone

jaws   unhinged   a hymen of teeth   and venus to colonize.

melanin deepening   and shallowing like   a bathtub
treat   for adventurous men   to soak in
without drowning.

men
try on new shades of women   like new pairs   of shoes
think our skin   tanned   to be   his soles

men want to pinpoint   which continents I connect
dissect   strange amalgamation into   prey   clearer
to the bordering eye

when he says   he only wants   mixed   babies
he's saying   he wants his daughter to be   fuckable
and lighter   than his lunch bag

he posted his order up   a while ago
we   are   late serving   his cocktail heritage   to him
custom   how one orders a piece
of meat: medium
rare   mantled
trophy   animal, jaw

unhinged, too deep

to drown.

Hair

i twist strands into the bellybuttons of roses
reconstitute them into a tiara on my scalp
consider cutting off the bulbs but

remember a photo of child me floating in the bathtub
hair flayed out, a thick net
holding both
my mother and my father
waving

What to Do on Bad Days

become comfortable with silence
welcome your confessions through the front door this time
they have missed being treated as guests
and not intruders

I Shave While Listening to Warsan Shire

My thighs do not skim soft
and white, like milk.

Texture roughened and spoiled
the razor some time ago.

In eighth grade, my resolution was to wear short-shorts like the pretty girls for
once. So in my room, I clutched my mother's razor and sheared away every
impolite black hair on my armpits, thighs, calves, navel, stomach,
in preparation for a retreat on female empowerment.

Now, I hold a fistful of pubic hair
mangled like a magpie's nest of kindling
as Warsan Shire recites through my phone,

"My beauty is not beauty here."

I am not under the microscope of a racist patriarch, I'm in my room. Alone in
this ritual again, but gripping my own heirloom this round, shrill and sharp in
the way only bitches can hear. Still thinking my pussy ain't pink enough to bite
back, floundering in the purgatory between feminist gallery and front-page porn.
And this is what the boys (yes, and the men) never want want to know,

how women of color
shear, pluck, press, wax, bleach
ourselves ripe until nothing is left
but inoffensive peach fuzz and a clear landing strip for bruises
to scrape until wet and smooth.

Where can my beauty survive
long enough to call itself by name?

Conditions of acceptance keep spilling
through keyhole of my sanctuary. This is not a victory story. The men's eyes
start looking like the body-posi litanies, like the feminist mantras, they start
looking like my sisters', I am still shearing myself polite under the soundtrack of
empowerment, Ms. Shire,

their eyes look like mine.

For Claudette Colvin

"I think you brought the revolution to montgomery" –Reverend Johnson

you braided head of oil / you cup runneth over with glue / you squeaked rally cry and stubborn psalms / your shoulders weighed two angels, sojourner and harriet / you lost to history's loud lock on cell door / you too shrill and dark for movement march / you fire in the night / you limped name for constitutional right / you sweet, abandoned girl / you cruel rite of passage / you swelled belly of shame / you respectable only in retrospect / history owes your books and girlhood back / owes you a seat while you're still here.

Missing Persons Report Filed for the Knife of Charleena Lyles

*Charleena Lyles was a 30-year-old black mother of four who called to report a
burglary and was shot dead by two white Seattle police officers after allegedly
threatening them with a knife. Neither officer used the de-escalation tactics they
had been trained with. They are still employed by SPD.*

police
glanced her tongue & saw blade
conjured knife
from the cockiness
of her throat dare breathe
saw vertebrae of her quaking spine
/ grenade keys
mistook her words
as / gunpowder
every
blink
a
/ trigger
she
pregnant ticking
/ bomb.

8. COMPLIANCE WITH SPD USE OF FORCE POLICY	
3. Compliance with the SPD Use of Force policy:	If "No", then:
a. Was the force used Reasonable, Necessary, and Proportional? ☐Yes ☐No b. Did the force conform to all policy requirements? ☐Yes ☐No	☐ Refer to OPA. Specific policy violations referred:
Board Analysis & Conclusions (each involved employee):	
SEE ATTACHED REPORT	
☐ Deferred to pending OPA Investigation	

away from Ms. Lyles ("at conversational length") looking down and writing notes relating to the
reported burglary in his notebook, when he saw Ms. Lyles' hand suddenly move from her right
side:

Um, as I was looking down to write um, I believe it was, I was gonna write the PlayStation
4 that she had just mentioned, um I noticed her arm moving uh her hand um um that
was by her side uh, I don't know if it was in her pocket or where, where her hand was
exactly as I was writing um, I saw (unintelligible), a f-, a flash of a, a knife, uh you know a
blade coming directly at my, towards my abdomen and uh as you know like a sticking
motion, her arm was coming straight out and towards me, towards my abdomen with
um what I saw was a knife um, it appeared to be maybe, maybe a 4 or 5 inch knife, I don't
recall exactly how long it was in that brief second.

He described:

At that moment I was kind of, kind of in, in shock about you know, that she was talking
normally and interacting with us normally and then all of a sudden she's trying to stab me
with a knife. And uh, I remember jumping back and uh, uh kinda fumbling back and the,
the door's right behind me. Um, and uh just the look on her face changed completely
focused on me like
Um, our conversation was very cordial and, uh, it was, you know, just the standard,   face the change to
standard conversation you have with anybody. Um, you know, it was back and forth. I
was asking her questions and she was answering and, uh, she didn't appear st- odd or
any-, you know, nothing stood out to me that, you know, was different, you know. Her
children were playing on the floor and, um, yeah, I mean everything seemed, seemed
normal, you know, as far as her behavior and everything during the conversation, so.

seattle police call this nightmare-making
"Training Policy"

(using a taser "wasn't protocol".
"hands on approach" would have
"put them at risk"
pepper spray was "tactically counterproductive"
could have endangered
the officer's ability
to
breathe.)

"There was no viable alternative,"
department says,
besides twisting her body—black & alive—
into a banshee

a black woman's body
is always gleaned more weapon
than mother
as if nothing
can harvest here but
husks of babies
& bullets.

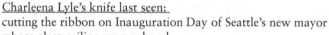

<u>Charleena Lyle's knife last seen:</u>
cutting the ribbon on Inauguration Day of Seattle's new mayor
whose glass-ceiling womanhood
— like her title "trailblazer" —
is also steeped in whiteness.

Officer Anderson reported that he sucked in his abdomen and jumped back to avoid being stabbed, dropping his notebook, which was later located at the scene on the floor in the apartment. He reported that he drew his department-issued Glock 9 mm handgun, directed her to "Get back!"

Ms. Lyles fell to the ground, landing on the floor in the entrance to the kitchen. Her infant child, who had been crawling around the living room, climbed on to her back. Officer McNew radioed "Shots fired. The subject is down. We need officers on scene. We need medics as well. We are not under control." At that point, Ms. Lyles' older son, whom officers had not known to be in the apartment, opened the door to the bedroom, in which he had reportedly been sleeping. Officer McNew asked him to go back into the room.

<u>Charleena's knife last seen:</u>
cutting the limestone of this
Glittering Republic
skyscraper
by
skyscraper
headstones in a city she might
have once called hers
but would never hug
her back

Both officers independently made their decisions to fire their duty weapons. Casings and bullets recovered at the scene and bullets recovered during autopsy show that Officer Anderson fired four rounds and Officer McNew fired three.

When asked whether he believed he had any alternatives to the use of force, Officer Anderson stated in part: "There was no time. We didn't have any shielding and we didn't have any distance between us. There was ... literally feet between us." Officer McNew stated: "At the point where I decided to use force, as I explained before, the subject had unabated access to me, to my person, and she was armed. I didn't feel that there was any other reasonable alternative."

Officer McNew further explained his thought process:

<u>Charleena's knife last seen:</u>
haunting the guilt of officers & a city too infatuated
with its own reflection
to see her
gleaming in the corners of
their Trumped-up nightmares.

Q. Okay. Was, prior to her attempted, or her assault on you, was, uh, she a suspect in any kind of a crime?

A: No.

Q. That you know of at that time.

A: No.

Q: So did she give you any, uh, reason to—in your mind—to pat her down, to frisk her?

A: No, there was no need. She was a complainant, she was calling to report a burglary that had occurred in her apartment. There's no reason you would ask her to keep her hands out or, you know, anything like that, you know. Um, we're going to take her,

Seattle,
after all,
only has so much patience
for those who are black AND angry
whose trauma longer than a soundbite
and a week of headlines

"how awful they must feel," someone pale & alive tells me,
"to have killed someone by mistake. To have to live with that."

                                    police brutality ain't supposed to happen here, right?
                                                not in this safe space city
                                                its liberals are so heartbroken.
                 too bad their bleeding hearts don't feed justice, just-stain hands.
                 too bad their guilt never makes it to the courthouses, somehow.
                                  "too bad" "too bad" too bad"

Charleena's knife last seen:
cutting umbilical cord of
uniformed men
babied by a society that will always
call their fist an open palm
who will never teach them how to pronounce
a c c o u n t a b i l i t y
in front of a mirror

"maybe they feel guilty,
but she's still dead," I say.

REVIEW OF INCIDENT SUPERVISION–*List by Each Involved Supervisor*	
Administrative Approval: The review board finds that the supervision and direction of the incident appears to be consistent with policy and training.	
Administrative Disapproval: The review board finds that the supervision and direction of the incident does not appear to be consistent with policy or training. See above for analysis details.	
Name and Serial Number	**Approved / Disapproved / Deferred to OPA**
1. A/Sgt. Schroeder, T. #6900	Approved
2. A/Lt. Pieper, P. #5335	Approved
3. A/Lt. Simmons, C. #6347	Approved
4. Lt. Arata, J. #5258	Approved
5. Lt. Fitzgerald, D. #6152	Approved
6. Capt. Sano, E. #4824	Approved

Missing Persons Report for the Words I Did Not Say:
I CAN'T MAKE IT
THROUGH AN ARTICLE ABOUT THE SHOOTING
WITHOUT CRYING
AND STILL, NOTHING HAS BEEN DONE

Last seen:
shattering every liberals,
heart of glass
& blood too dark
to bring up at dinner.
GUESS WHAT?
YOU'RE REELING FROM THE KICKBACK OF A GUN
YOU DON'T EVEN KNOW YOU SHOT.

Charleena Lyles is still dead.
Seattle thrives & she is still dead.
I perform this poem & she is still dead
Mayor sharpens her reputation on her headstone at the MLK rally & she is still dead
Police try holding her knife
up to a mirror
it shrivels into ash
yet she is still dead.

she is still dead.
she is still dead.

UOFRB Chair / Assistant Chief	Date	Print Name	Serial	Unit #
L. CORDNER	12/7/17	A/C Cordner	5432	C100

Vigil

Faced with no other option, I pray

heaven is the old Station, cramped
pressure cooker of community.
Let their stage be the top of its well-loved staircase,
tall as a lighthouse guiding fearless rowboats home.

Heaven is an eternal cypher, its gates open with their snap.
Heaven has one of those rolley office chairs
(like the one in our favorite teacher's room)
and it's always their turn to be spun around.

There is always someone to listen in heaven.
There is a forest of listeners who fall and are heard.

Someplace softer, they invite us for a walk on the beach.
In this place, there is play, and if they want,
they are new.
They try every shortened dream on for size
and it fits.

They try on new names, new theories freckled with stars.
In heaven, the aliens only want their company.

I pray they wake up in a kinder heaven.
I pray they always call shotgun and the aux cord.
I pray there are no police,
no writers block in heaven,
that whenever their mouth begins to form an apology,
it sings their name instead.

In this softer place,
they are living out the rest of summer:
smogless, extraordinary,
singing.

What To Do on Bad Days

you have lost nothing and have nothing to lose
the best parts of yourself are still intact
they live in the gardens you tend
you reap what you sow
don't mourn a past harvest or phases after they have waned
they will come back around like an old friend eventually
don't worry, you are not expiring

Flamin Hot Royalty.

after Anastacia Reneé

Gold dust fingers to royal
to pick up anything of our own.
Gleeful clap, hands joined at the fingertips, we waste nothing
suck our teeth and then our fingers clean.

Pinkies up, we are flamin hot royalty,
in the back of our mama's car
the days we threw a wish of $2 and a pitstop
down her earlobe driving home.

in the schoolyard where suddenly we become popular,
gold dust spreading invisible like pollen.
Dozens of finger soldiers bowing at our bounty.
Dozens of bees buzzing about our crunchy harvest
and mama always taught me to share,
just like everyone else's mama
taught them to share so together,
we have a bottomless crop.

It's always summer somewhere in some kid's dimples,
smile cracking a horizon crisp as Arizona tea
(which never ages out of being 99 cents).
Sun red, proud, and blazing
eager to taste
all this adolescent season
can offer.

Birthright

The first summer Seattle was choked by smog
my hands swung at my sides, fingers butter-knifed
through the congested air as I hurried through Cap Hill.
I want you to remember the sun,

melting push-pop orange and hazy, how it stuck out in the hot grey
like a vengeful Auntie God's gaudy christmas ornament.
I want you to remember that summer. How when anyone wore a filter mask,
someone always said it looked like Mad Max and how the air quality was
        "just as bad as Asia",
like the fires hadn't always been our stifled next door neighbors,
like our ports are not tetris boards of demanded-discarded imports.

Now, all across the world the sunsets leak,
spilling their lava lamp red across open sore waters.

In living memory is the smogless summers,
when the sun was Auntie God's ethereal basketball dribbling through days
varsity-bright and gleaming. When we got too hot, we ran through the heavenly arch
of the garden hose and shook like puppies before setting ourselves out to dry,
only then to charge into oceans on a dare like the waves
weren't trying to push us back
to our mothers.

Now, I clutch the old world in my fist like beach glass.
I, too, have been rounded soft by the privilege of water.

Did children ask to outgrow their oceans?
Is it just up to us to dig new wells?

I collect tinted memories like purple clam shells, only for them to rot
in a jar on my windowsill. When asked to write about environmentalism and hope,
I tried skipping seasonal nostalgia on a desperate sea like a hollowed stone.
But it fell flat and sank.

Next summer will be choked by smog.
I cut a pinhole in my water bill and see this new world trickling into ours.
it's pricks like dry pine needles but we can make it festive,
a little gaudy if we're lucky.

This new world is not as abundant as it used to be,
but it is wiser,
and that's what matters.

There's new summer jams to be made here, from windchimes made of fish hooks
and storms filtered through bleached factory engines,
millions of retired hearts lining the old viaduct,
lining the abandoned oil pipeline, former splitting image of America hollowed into flute
flowing through the countryside sighing one
long
apology.

"Birthright" is no longer synonymous with colonizing every body of water with
            our garbage
while forcing its faucets to run for as long as we please. So we walk to the river
and it welcomes our shaking knees.

I pick up bottle cap hills and the last shards of sea glass.
I work for forgiveness, but never
freedom from consequence.

Can you see next summer rising?
Can you feel us outgrowing the privilege of our ports?

This smog
brings so many new colors.
Let us make the best of them.

Tahlequah

In the summer of 2018, Tahlequah the orca carried her dead calf
for 17 days across the Salish sea in an unprecedented tour of mourning.

On her head, balances an oranging limp
promise of a golden child.

I think of how many mothers
have crossed oceans for their children
while begging them to float on shrinking fat.

Drink enough salt water
and you can feel whole bestiaries below the surface.
Empty cradles of white coral, saline dripping
tides of the endangered meeting streams of the extinct.

Estuaries of ghosts, tangled in saltmarsh
mourned by gambled tracking chips,
expensive brunches,
and museum plaques.

"Extinct"
is just the blameless elegy version of
"exterminated."

The floods on the other side of the country will never reach our sounds.
Quiet ripples, the ugly guilt we sink to the bottom of the Pacific,
the rusted stomachs of gulls
the singing bowls we kick in the bleached summer sand.

Farmed salmon engulf the sea in a tsunami of net and steel.
A clanging lullaby in the slitting of a fat, orange underbelly,

a (de)crescendo of scales,
into the blackening water.

Bowl

Under pressure, I tan my palms
two brazen, tender basins.

In the crease quartering my pointer finger from my thumb,
drip sinew and mercury.

It takes an hour to pull this consolation prize
of a mind out of bed or office chair.

I chew silk worm cocoons over morning coffee.
Throughout the day, I pull tattered scarves out my throat like a magician.

I fight fear for hours.
Come back from this backdrop battle, numb and acidic.

In a veteranless war, I am the crown princess of tired.
I come from the land of cut wicks and dried clay.

My corrosive, impatient rage
is a plugged tea kettle of halogens.

I search for a mute canary
in a forest of coal mines.

I scold my skittish shadow
running from its mother's light.

I hope you, too, have fantasized about crying in front of people.
I curve my spine into a waiting bowl.

This architecture of fear
I'll build myself a castle,
I swear.

What to Do on Bad Days

don't mistake emptiness as a meal
practice finding comfort outside of surrender

what do i do

when the rituals stop answering
my calls? when all the podcasts i've listened to
don't metamorphosize me into a productive person?
i still feel unloved
after someone tries to love me once with three (3) heart emojis;
all the affirmations sound corny;
my commitments sound like failed attempts to blow a symphony
thru a split blade of grass. the biggest victory i had today
was not splitting blade on skin. what do i do when my healing isn't "ig" worthy?
you have stopped listening by now; i'm so ~grounded~
every limb becomes an anchor drowning in a dead sea;
i treat my mouth an open wound and scab it shut;
what do i do when i run out of metaphors for pain, you applaud me?
when i'd rather disappear than be resilient? the most inspiring reason i have to
be resilient is work in the morning. what do i do when depression memes just
aren't funny anymore?

what do i do when the audiences get bored?
when my joint insecurities become "stop copying me" wailed between two mirrors?
what do i do when i reach for the pen and all that sputters out are old poems?
if i still don't have happy endings for them?
they ask for closure and all i have is shoestrings dangling
from open wires. what do i do when i call on the ancestors
but forget
i'm in a different time zone? when i'm lost in translation?
what do i do when when i regret the poems as I'm writing them?
i can't stand my own company, i still hate myself after the workshop.
what do i do if they forget my voice?
when the youth poet prodigy gimmick expires? when they forget me,
what will i have left?

Womanhood Speaks to Patriarchy Uninterrupted for the First Time

the whole time you withheld your love from me I waited.

found one hundred different knots for my tongue.
sewed a chain of pawnshop rings
molded a makeshift Eve from wax, sipped glass like water
& hung mirrors on every wall.

i confessed my sins
to the corner i assigned myself in your absence.
counted every calorie & word wasted
trying to reel you in without pulling too desperate
i would've loved myself first
but that would have been unfaithful

so instead i shrank
& i shrank
& shrank
until forgiveness
nestled a tumor
in the cradle of my hips
& i said

"thank you."

even though
i asked to be
human

YOU MADE ME
"WOMAN"
INSTEAD.

PATRIARCHY, WHERE DO I BEGIN

My first word was "**no**"
so the second one you taught me was
"*sorry*"
I remember learning the word
"**sister.**"
tentatively calling her's
my own,
my daughter's
innocence
"*girlhood*"
while you called it your fetish

everything always has to be sexy for you to listen so I made my body a megaphone
hollow & amplifying

I learned that for women,
ugly
is short for
worthless
so I trained every bone in my body
to bend pretty so one day,
slim & sharp enough,
I can cough one up like a swallowed key
unlock privilege from the femininity
you forced me to stomach

sometimes
I wrap my arms around my body
and find my fingers
grasping at helium
you always want me to sound higher
be lighter than air itself
be only defined
by your shapes
I fill

when you are not looking, i put on my face everyday
come home and wash it down the drain.
pick apart whatever is between my legs for you
like "this is woman enough"
"this isn't."
You twisted sisterhood into a rat race.
now, i look at them and see only what i do not have.

I need **you** like i need air
when you're holding my head underwater
telling me to liberate myself at the same time

Patriarchy, my sisters are dying
& you are always mistaking their blood as lipstick stains
you only seem to care when they have your last name.

To be woman
means to be blamed for your own casket
and I'm
tired
of funerals so I learned
Feminism

Will you love this feminism when it is not pretty?
Will you be so eager to hashtag my movement when it does not turn you on?

Will you love me when I am not pretty?
Will you love me when I do not turn you on?

I know you've made progress, Patriarchy
on some occasions, you've even raised your fist with us but
even your most progressive heroes
come home to beat me.

I am done waiting for you to love me back
I'm taking every hour spent silent and screaming
to fill balloons at the party I throw for me & my sisters
and you will not invite yourself this time

It'll be so luxurious
so redemptive
your God is gonna foot the bill,
every mirror is gonna shatter
we'll forgive
on our own time
and
there you'll be

waiting.

Medusa Becomes an Instagram Model

In feminist movements, Medusa is a symbol of monstrous female rage.
Medusa is also the logo of luxury fashion brand Versace.

She became the *baddest* bitch
on your explore page
Stone cold gaze placated by filter.
Every rough edge exfoliated
into softer fragments of her gavel

gargled down with Fit Tea,
stone tumbled smooth
by waist trainer.

When she hissed, her lips pursed into pout,
snakes an exotic bouquet of curls.
So fierce, how she petrified our gawks.

For fear of seeing her own reflection,
the photographers shot Medusa
through an elaborate configuration
of mirrors.

Everyone wants the heaven of beauty
but no one wants to grind
their pain into capstone.

Cut all offenses that portrude, hang, and scar.
Contour and seal yourself into grace, immortal and
creaseless.

When Medusa finally angled the camera
towards herself for the first time,
she froze into statue.

First death
by selfie.
Monument
of vanity.

Medusa was featured in an exhibit.
People stared, and stared, and stared.
Chipped away every unsexy ripple of
ugly, every sedimentary layer of age.

Most stunna icon.
Baddest bitch
in legend.

Her followers said
Slayyyyy
when Perseus paraded her scalp

down Wall Street,
swung her by the limp serpents, edges
skinned off.

While on the sidelines of the catwalk,
as the rest of her body crumbled
into sediment,

her followers congratulated Perseus
on his new collection:
the Hermes gold-winged sandals,
the helm of invisibility,
Hephaestus's sword.

Said her decapitated head
on his shield was
such a statement
piece.

What to Do on Bad Days

You said the wrong thing and elegance drops
and breaks into a thousand irreparable shards
it is a luxury you can't afford
but you've always been frugal, anyway
try not to be tempted by sharp things
that hurt when you hold them.

Palanquin .

I parade my identity in a palanquin of headless men.

I dance and swear
upon your sabotaged stage.

I jump through your hoops
wielding a torch
aflame with hair!

I wear a garland of beheaded
smirks! I dance, a dozen
flailing arms on a white boy's chest.

I am a fearfully worshipped Gen Z deity.
Every generation
I wake in a tide of Black

wake up one white flesh
–pound stronger, my praise
is a long time
coming.

Wherever your gut wrenches and your mouth
stitches shut, I am there
pummeling bitterness to a pulp.

I bought your silence with the currency of my swallowed cries.
My mercy birthed
your supremacy.

I never die!
I only take a self care day,
nice try.

I am the shrillest
in a ballroom of suit-clad words
my naked palm the sharpest weapon
against systems so
loud they became a
hum.

I am who is needed and you spit in my face.
You threw yourself at the feet of change and blamed
her for crushing you.

I return your demagogue son's body to sender.
I cut your daughter's white pearls into intersectional pieces, watch her weep
white guilt on my red bottoms,
please.

I am reborn every generation in the voice of your youngest child,
in the decaying underbelly of the lion.

I emerge a pillar of salt and shade,
a cheap glimmering wig,
a sharpened trident of seeing,
hearing,
spitting evil when you
smothered my revenge for eons.

If you propose to me and ask
I get on my knees as prenup
I will scream
"NO!"
in the restaurant

I will smear ugly and
untamable on your diamonds
and take all the lonely girls out dress shopping.

Just try to test me then.
I will make this revolution an irresistible dance.

If you can't keep up,
get out the way.

Allegiance

Dear America,

as much as you believe your walls
are the only foundations I need,
I still have faith in other nations.

To begin, I pledge allegiance to my papa,
whose embrace feels like continents.

I pledge allegiance to the girls on Instagram
who gas each other up in every selfie.

I pledge allegiance to the heart eyes emoji
and its star-spangled cousin.

I pledge allegiance to la tienda on the corner by the train,
sheltering kids who just don't want to go home yet.

I pledge allegiance to The Station and the murals in SoDo,
to the Soufend, to northwest summer lakes still cold
as my brother implodes its tides.

I pledge allegiance to the last brave gulp of air
before someone learns to swim.

I pledge allegiance to libraries,
and everywhere else left where you don't have to pay to exist.

I pledge allegiance to the cocooning tent city on town hall's lawn,
to the requests blasting outside the youth jail on New Years.

I pledge allegiance to the external battery friend
and the bus drivers who wait.

America, I am not starved of faith.
America, these, too, are nations in repair of you.

America, I need the diligence of a "did you get home safe?" text.
I need justice not hung by a price tag.
I need patriotism that's more than a stiletto
on someone else's' pulse.

America, you have left the porch light off
far too many times,
that you are running out of chances
to convince me you are still home.

I do not worship your tyranny or want to fill its shoes either.
My poetry is the mouse at the foot of your elephant,

I will leave you running
humbled,

knowing we grew someplace brighter
where your walls once
trampled.

Allegiance 2

I don't have a name
for the change that's happening yet,

just know I'll be there,
juggling the pearls in my shoes
as I sharpen my oyester knife on the mountain.

I'll sit this squirming nation
between my mama's knees,
the bristle brush scraping a pink trail
down its coaxed neck.

I will dare this nation to move its head an inch
before it makes its transformation,
take any longer,
be any more painful than

it already is.

What To Do on Bad Days.

pause often
stop on a highway overpass
and watch the road below
it is the vein of a creature
greater than yourself
it breathes
and you are humbled
you exhale
and continue
with purpose

Diaspora

If the meaning of the prayer was not passed down to you,
find it through holier means than translation.
Cling to the rhythm instead.

If you were not taught the rhythm, memorize the clang
of knife against yam against wooden cutting board.
Keep it ringing, ringing in your ears.

If not the ring,
then the Bombay jazz club
and its green lanterns swaying in the long, long night

If you were not given the religion, then at least
hold Boompa's rosary beads,
their 5 finger-tipped memories
indented in thick amber,
the gold Zarathustra hanging from a neck
and tattooed on a sunburnt back.

If the traditions were never taught to you,
then cling to tea time always served at 2pm.
Display the cups and remember
elders do not take their tea with sugar,
like you do.

You have only a fraction of their blood.
You thicken your water with milk.

If home did not fit in the carry on compartment,
then the sprigs of lemongrass from the garden will do.
The tea bags brought from India will do.
The reusable garland will do.

The passport's golden lions
show a compass of 3 directions.
The fourth will do, too.
Its back facing you,
open jaws facing the homeland.

If the orthodox genealogy did not show up to the altar
of any of the son's weddings, identity still celebrates
the melting pot mothers. Inheritance
becomes the grateful garland
around the brownish baby's plump smile.

Her laughter, an anthem.
Her heartbeat, a golden rhythm.

Diaspora (cont.)

Grandfather praises Trader Joe's
instant butter chicken.

When we didn't have the right red paste
for his birthday sagan, we used lipstick

and it worked just fine.

Diaspora 3

don't you know America welcomed me with ice,

    and I still carved it into shelter?
Heaving hot water into a tub
               I rebaptized myself into
               a harder syllable? All so you could
megaphone when you
          want to?
   don't you know how   hard I worked?

   the fortunes I paid the lawyer? hoarded under our shaking table, disappearing
and   reappearing like frost? I have never stopped moving for 20 years for fear of
freezing   over,
         of being plowed over the border? I don't understand why
       it takes so long for you
        to get out   of bed. Can't you see the clock ticking? Can't you
feel   America choking   every   minute from   your   leisure
       like I can?

         Don't you know how hard I work? Don't you know I love   you?
     That's   why I'm   always reminding   you
what   more   my blood
is capable   of   doing?

         Don't you know   the languages   I lost
      to make it here? How all this   time,   America still   hasn't
swallowed   me
           whole?

Portraits of Wayne

1.   Photo album

- *wasted genius*
- *atlanta office*
- *chess board in washington park*
- *finance degree*
- *tan lines in brazil*
- *faded seahawks shirt*
- *hugging my grandmother's shoulders*
  from behind, her hands two swans
  cradling his arms
- *laying on a bed with my grandmother*
  and baby uncle, his chubby hand on his father's thigh,
  laughing
- *triptych of high school portraits*
  mailed to sisters and cousins,
  all returned at some point
  to make it to this folder.

2.   How do you mourn an absent father?

> *(They say he was a kind and pleasant man,*
> *just a little weird.*
> *He wasn't mean.*
> *He used to win chess tournaments blindfolded in central park—*
> *mom considered it a victory if she managed to get 5 moves in.*
> *We never had a chance for a rematch.)*

When I was 4, I met with in South Carolina.
I remember staring under the bridge at a crawfish.
Everyone called it an autumn leaf but I knew better.
Mom says, "you believed so hard it was that thing that it was,
that it was."

If I believe hard enough that we were family,
then we were.

3.   Inheritance

Grandfather is a foggy absence
in my kidneys, history
trickles from an orphaned abscess.

Family is South of splits I haven't mended,
funerals I've never attended.
My great aunt's gravestone, polyped by marigolds,
fragile legacies carved from lyme, prayer, and distance.

Photo albums of faces
I know only through features and not voices.
Columbariums of cheeks, smiles, and noses
a lineage full of plot holes,
phantom limbs and abandoned
next of kins.

4.   In a stroke of tragic irony, we see him in our smiles.

(he died from kidney failure
from being a crack addict for 40 years ~~he used to fall asleep in the middle of the~~
~~floor in the middle of the day in the middle of~~ ▮▮▮▮ ~~life he gave her~~ ▮
▮▮▮▮▮▮▮ ~~and to her it felt like pennies~~ *you can't buy back lost time, you*
can't buy back lost daughters)

She has his cheeks and I have her cheeks.
When our cheeks bubble with laughter,
they become two fat dumpling coins below our chevron eyes.
Smiles worth millions, smiles worth a degree in economics,
a smile worth a sweet vow of family and revolution

5.   Rage

WHO WOULD WE BE WITHOUT THESE SYSTEMS?
WHO COULD WE HAVE BEEN WITHOUT WHITE SUPREMACY'S
SABOTAGE?
IF WE CAME FIRST AND STAYED THERE?

6. Bronze

Grandma says she cried the Nile for that man for decades.
Says we are bronze statues with mud feet,
we have all this brilliance but still must eat.

I find myself sinking in Carolina rivers,
my chest a drowned singing bowl
(w)ringing lost names for inheritance.

My feet, two waterlogged cymbals
clambering towards porch light mirages
on the dark side of the warmth of other suns,

will-o-wisking away daughters
who leash their sons from dark waters
fearing they can't be buoys in their bloodlines, fearing one hit will turn them
inside out and leave them too breathless to want to come up for air again,
fearing addiction will hug them like an outcast relative insisting on being
remembered, and not want to come back home again.

What third place luck.
What an undeserving curse.

7. We can't be mad at him forever

my grandfather was schizophrenic.
I heard someone can live with schizophrenia dormant
in them for years,
but it can be triggered by traumatic events.
mom told me when he did the sit ins
at the segregated diners, an officer shoved his gun
in his mouth.

He self-medicated. In hospice, he thought he was a pharaoh. Is dying thinking
you were heirless royalty a blessing or a curse? Is there peace for a king that
outcast his kingdom?

8.   Five person funeral + body

There is a tense distance
between calling a family member by their name
instead of their title.
He morphed from Wayne into my grandfather
in the manner of cremation.

Sacrilegious pharaoh crypt, schizophrenic iv drip, driest re-baptism; chalked up
red dirt and ashed kidney, condensed inheritance
resting
on our windowsill.

Now, he can never leave home again.

What to Do on Bad Days

you are frustrated with yourself because you are contradictory
but that just means you are strong enough
to be the home for many things

AlphaZero vs. Stockfish 8: Longterm Sacrifice

I'll be a cymballed knight sent out
to a slumbering war.

I'll play the queen you
refuse to crown and
skip over pixelated trenches,
touting the rook by his
strewn, white collar

I'll haunt like a besieged castle
my remnants raise themselves
wherever you turn your back.
I'll move forward at a pace
you will never match.

I'll beckon you to me, voiceless king,
clinging to your throne in your rusting age.

I am a hustling, impatient heir.
I'll shed my tenderness and become invincible
then you'll see me then
you'll see me see me then you'll see me and
I won't even need you.

Pedagogy

I regret grafting apologies to my brother's skin
and pretending they are the only armor he can afford.

What else can I teach him than to swallow his anger
when there are bullets
waiting for an excuse on our doorstep?

What else can I teach him than to shrink
when white people misjudge him as a giant?
Twist his reaching fingers into fists? Emmett Till a body
he's just now growing into. Don't they know he was a baby,
drooling on my lap not that long ago?
Now he is one inch shorter than me
and growing faster than safety can keep up.

I regret every time I have told my sister to stop crying,
to evaporate her tears until they are more salt
than water until she,
a growing ocean of bitter,
tries drowning all the tides that show her softness.

A black girl's pain is only worth as much as it claps back,
but ain't we doing them a favor?

Giving them a structure more forgiving than a chalk outline?
White supremacy ain't gonna keep on the light on.
Ain't gonna count to ten when you can't lullaby the bullet.

It takes a village to raise a child,
to discipline every misstep as not to invite the fall.

We are taught to not cast shadows bigger than we are,
to take up the least space possible in a world
unconvinced by our innocence.

I am of this village.
Whenever my temper snaps, my voice
irritated and impulsive,
becomes the sirens in my siblings' heads.

The belt, the lock and never the key.
I have taught them so well to quiet
when they leave the house,
they shrink inside of it too.

Like telling my brother to stop running up and down the street to burn off steam
because his sneakers flying off the pavement is a sudden movement, and when he
turns the corner
I can't see what's waiting for him.

Like my sister and her tenderness need to grow up already,
as I rip her hand from my sleeve, ignoring
what made her hold it in the first place.

How many generations until we are born
unafraid?
Until we can afford a pedagogy
of gentleness?

My sister
keeps the light on until I come home.
My brother
always opens the door.

What To Do on Bad Days

your body is already forgiving you
your charred palms are becoming soft
and strong enough to hold things again
you have a talent for melting like wax,
and wandering for a form to take
on bad days

you reconstruct yourself with patience

Elevator Pitch for Happy Poem

okay, so somewhere, there is someone actin a fool for their crush and one day, about a year from now (we can write this too), they will look back and laugh in the tone of wind chimes
ringing from a closed door.

And then, we cut to a scene where someone is making a playlist for their lover. Each song is the soundtrack to a fantasy unrolling as slick as the rainbow sheen of a cd and then, someone who has been hiding love under their tongue like a snuck candy pulls a confession out of the cookie jar of someone else's love and they laugh and laugh and laugh.

In another scene, someone
- moves a snail to the other side of the sidewalk instead of stepping on it
- pretends not to know a fact so they could learn it from a child thrilled to be the expert for the first time
- compliments an insecurity that winds its first twirl in a mirror
- learns a new secret handshake and tries—really, really hard—to remember it for next time
- kisses a forehead—a wound we can't see—better
- triumphs over a bad habit and starts stumbling into the yellow brick road of healthy

and hear me out on this scene:
there is no sadness suckerpunching the credits in this one.

Pain has always been invited
actually, it's been a protagonist the whole time.
We just never looked in its face long enough
to see the cathartic break in its shrinking pupils

I mean,
sadness has always been the other half of the seesaw,
without it there would be no game of swing.

I want to push every button and insist
the low-budget beauty in this world is still worth scouting for
and yeah, I see you're trying to get off the elevator
but don't you see?

You keep tucking joy behind your ear
like you're waiting for the right trick
to pull it out.

In the Event I Do Not Change the World

"From space I saw Earth—indescribably beautiful with the scars of national boundaries gone." —Muhammad Ahmad Faris, Syrian Astronaut, 1991

In elementary school, teachers encouraged us to be astronauts.
I will probably never make an appearance in their diversified STEM dreams
but I still imagine floating in the steel hull of a spaceship,
peering down at the world from behind a reinforced window,

looking down at this small, revolving body of tension
swaddled in thin atmosphere,
swinging on the vast, silent playground of space.

Squinting, I cannot see the explosions erupting on its skin,
but the growing pains echo still.

In the event I do not change the world,
but help raise it instead,

I hold its hand as it skips over fault lines cracked in the street.
Help it chop an onion the way my aunties taught me:
to hold water on my tongue so I cry less, to thank
the puddle of privilege without breaking fast.

I listen to the world's grief and musings on the porch swing,
the bus ride back home,
the pockets of time after class.

I celebrate every one of its questions
and transcribe a holy book of its answers.

I invite it on stage to play
when it has been captive audience its entire life.
I dull its sharp instruments when I say goodnight.

One day, inevitably,
I will get so exhausted with how the world keeps hurting itself
over and over,
I will turn my back on it.

We will orbit each other in restorative circle.
From the gravity,
accountability forms in our hands.

We learn how to hold this star together.
We bury the guns in the dry dirt.

I will likely not make it to space,
but I do not need a dramatic launch to view the world swinging
—a heavy pendulum—
from where I am standing now.

I am not begging to be known.

When I knock over the false heroes,
trust it is because the world needs room for better ones.

I raise that justice is not a gentle word.
"Equity" and "Love" are not toothless either.
Spinning in a carousel of dead ends,
whoever can afford to sleep at a crossroads
has never been chased from a border.

Trust, these are not times to tiptoe around the world
like it is sleeping undisturbed in a white cradle,
like its not daring to grow its orbit every day.

I may not change the world, but
I can stand up without fearing someone else will take my seat.
I can challenge and love the world, boundlessly.

I can sit at my own window and overview every crevice.
I can whisper into the terrestrial noise,
"still, there is change within my grasp."

What To Do on Bad Days

this is a poem that has no end.
it will keep going
just as we will.

Acknowledgments

Matt Gano and Aaron Counts, thank you for catching what my poems could do without and guiding them to the best versions they can be. Also, for line breaks. This book couldn't exist without you, the organizational wizard Alicia Craven, and the good folks at Seattle Arts and Lectures and Urban Word NYC.

Immense gratitude to my first and forever poetic homes: Youth Speaks Seattle and Nova High School for encouraging weird, beautiful poet kids to thrive.

Thank you to the first drafts of these poems and the ones that did not make it into *Stepwell*. Thank you 16, 17, and 18 year old Azura.

Thank you to Farhad Tyabji for being the most supportive father and weeknight chef I could ask for.

Thank you to Julia Ismael, my mother and inspiration to unpack the world's stories with thoughtful, gentle realness.

Thank you to my siblings Hafiz and Zainab for reminding me to laugh.

Thank you to my partner and my crew of friends who continually teach me what love can look like.

Thank you Arts Corps, who make my dream/destiny of being a teaching artist clearer every day, and let me exploit the hell out of the office printer to mark up every first draft.

Thank you to the wider poetry community of Seattle. You keep the artistic fabric and integrity of this city intact. I am so fortunate to grow up in your brimming landscape of slams, readings, open mics, writing circles, workshops, everything.

This community is a well of faith, energy, and love I pull from daily. Thank you for sustaining me.

About the Author

Azura Tyabji is a young Taurus of Black and Indian descent from Seattle, Washington. She is the 2018-19 Seattle Youth Poet Laureate and National Youth Poet Laureate Ambassador of the West Region of the United States. She strives to command attention to injustice and write a future without it into existence.

This book is set in Sabon

Book Design by Cara Sutherland
with assistance from
Lucas Wildner and Alexa Burkett

CPSIA information can be obtained
at www.ICGtesting.com
Printed in the USA
LVHW041508161020
669012LV00002B/339